Down by the River

Afro-Caribbean Rhymes, Games and Songs for Children

Compiled by Grace Hallworth • *Illustrated by* Caroline Binch

F

FRANCES LINCOLN
CHILDREN'S BOOKS

www.franceslincoln.com

To Harold Rosen, who started all this,
to Ann Gift, Tobago librarian, who aided and abetted,
and to all those who shared childhood memories – *G.H.*

For Deborah and Tobago's children – *C.B.*

Text copyright © Grace Hallworth 1996
Illustrations copyright © Caroline Binch 1996
The right of Grace Hallworth to be identified as the author and of Caroline Binch
to be identified as the illustrator of this work has been asserted by them
in accordance with the Copyright, Designs and Patents Act, 1988 (United Kingdom).

First published in Great Britain in 1996 by William Heinemann Ltd

This edition published in Great Britain 2010 and in USA in 2011 by
Frances Lincoln Children's Books, 4 Torriano Mews,
Torriano Avenue, London NW5 2RZ
www.franceslincoln.com

A catalogue record for this book is available from the British Library.

ISBN 978-1-84780-082-4

Printed in Heshan, Guangdong, China by Leo Paper Products Ltd in August 2010

1 3 5 7 9 8 6 4 2

INTRODUCTION

Most of the rhymes, songs, chants and lullabies that you will find in this book are ones that I remember from my childhood. Others have been contributed by friends from Trinidad or from other islands in the Caribbean.

I grew up in Trinidad and I remember my childhood as quite idyllic. I had three brothers and two sisters. Before I was eleven I had two homes. During the term I lived with my aunt who was a school teacher but at holiday times I lived at my parents' home.

It seems strange to describe my aunt's house as being near the sea – it was just eight streets away – because even now it seems far away. There were children in most of the houses round about (in our block there were three of us called Grace) so I had lots of friends.

Life at my aunt's house was ordered. There was music and adult conversation. I felt rather like an only child. Then, in the holidays, I was back in the noisy bustle of a larger family. At my parents' house boys' games predominated. My brothers taught me how to spin tops, pitch marbles, to whistle and to make up Robber talk, like the Midnight Robbers at Carnival time.

At high school I had the opportunity to meet children from many different backgrounds. We were a fantastic mix – Chinese, African, Asian, Portuguese, Spanish, English, Dutch, Jewish, French Creole, Syrian and many more, but although we represented so many races, our culture was the same – Trinidadian.

At the time, all these playground rhymes seemed ours alone. However, when I began to research them, I found that many of the singing and dancing games are European in origin, and that often the rhymes show traces of their French, African, English and American roots.

For me this is important. As children sing and play and then hand on the songs and games of their childhood, we see a living example of the inter-relationship of different cultures, and this is something for us all to appreciate and respect.

GRACE HALLWORTH

WAKE UP TIME

Pinchy, pinchy, pinchy,
Fly, fly away.

Birdy, birdy, birdy,
Fly, fly away.

Clap hands for Mamma,
Till Daddy come;
Daddy bring cake an' sugar plum
An' give baby some.

PLAYTIME

Down by the river,
Down by the sea,
Johnny break a bottle
An' he say is me.
I tell Ma,
Ma tell Pa,
Johnny get a licking,
An' a ha! ha! ha!

One potato, two potato,
Three potato, four,
Five potato, six potato,
Seven potato,
    More.

RAINY DAY RHYMES

Rain, rain,
Go to Spain,
And never come back
To Trinidad again.

Rain, rain,
Go away,
Come again;
Another day.

*June is the start of the rainy season and
the beginning of hurricane weather.*

June too soon,
July stand by,
August come it must.
September remember,
October all over.

In the Playground

One, two, three, four, five, six, seven,
All good children go to heaven;
The clock in heaven strikes eleven,
One, two, three, four, five, six, seven.

Out goes the lady with the see-saw hat,
O-U-T spells OUT,
And out goes you.

Ziggedy ziggedy marble stone,
Pointer pointer buff,
Buff ca-lay-lay,
Fee fee lay-lay,
Bim, bam, fire!

Ring-a-ding-ding,
The school bell ring,
Teacher knickers
Tie up with string.
String pop,
Knickers drop,
Teacher run out the room,
Cry-ing.

SKIPPING ROPE

Bupsi-ky-sico pindar shell,
Miss say bupsi-ky-sico pindar shell.
I love coffee, I love tea.
I love the girls and the girls love me.

Miss Sue, Miss Sue,
From out of Ballou,
She's having a party,
Chika boom,
Chika boom-boom-boom.
Let's do the tip-tap-toe.
Mamma's got the cold,
Pappa's got the flu,
I ain't lying,
And neither are you.
Sitting in the palace
Peeling white potatoes,
Sitting in the alley
Drinking Black Labels.
Listen to the clock go,
Chit-chit chi wa-wa,
Chit-chit chi wa-wa,
FREEZE!

CLAP HANDS

Mosquito one,
Mosquito two,
Mosquito jump in de callaloo.
Mosquito three,
Mosquito four,
Mosquito fly out de ol' man door.

Mosquito five,
Mosquito six,
Mosquito break up de ol' man bricks.

Mosquito seven,
Mosquito eight,
Mosquito open de ol' man gate.

Mosquito nine,
Mosquito ten,
Mosquito tickle de ol' man hen.

Callaloo is a spinach dish.

Choose Your Partner

This way, Valery,
That way, Valery,
This way, Valery,
All day long.

Here comes the pretty one,
Just like the other one,
Here comes the pretty one,
All day long.

This way, Valery,
That way, Valery,
This way, Valery,
All day long.

BROWN GIRL IN THE RING

This is a circle game with one child in the middle performing the actions.

There's a brown girl in the ring
Tra-la-la-la-la.
There's a brown girl in the ring
Tra la-la-la-la.
A brown girl in the ring,
Tra-la-la-la-la,
For she's sweet like a sugar
And a plum, plum, plum.

Now show me your motion,
Tra-la-la-la-la,
Now show me your motion,
Tra la-la-la-la,
Now show me your motion,
Tra-la-la-la-la.
For she's sweet like a sugar
And a plum, plum, plum.

Now hug and kiss your partner,
Tra-la-la-la-la,
Now hug and kiss your partner,
Tra la-la-la-la.
Now hug and kiss your partner,
Tra-la-la-la-la.
For she's sweet like a sugar
And a plum, plum, plum.

GOING SHOPPING

One day, one day,
Congotay.

I went down the bay,
Congotay.

I meet an ol' lady,
Congotay.

With a box of chickens,
Congotay.

I ask her for one,
Congotay.

But she wouldn't give me
Congotay.

She's a greedy Mamma,
Congotay.

So I took it anyway,
Congotay.

CONGOTAY is an alternating chant in which two lines of children stand, Indian file, with the leader (Mamma) of one side protecting the children (her chickens) behind her.

I diggin' potatoes,
  John belly gros.

All roun' de harbour,
  John belly gros.

An' coo coo in de fire,
  John belly gros.

An' de cat can't catch me,
  John belly gros.

*Coo coo is a dish of corn meal and
okra cooked in butter.*

FRIENDSHIPS

Blue blue,
Your love is true.
Red red,
You wet your bed.
Green green,
You eat ice cream.
Pink pink,
You smelling stink.
Yellow yellow,
You kiss a fellow.
White white,
You fly a kite.
Brown brown,
You go to town
In your dirty washekong.
Black black,
You break my back.

Washekong are trainers.

TAUNTS AND TEASES

Tit for tat,
Butter for fat;
You kill m' dog,
I go kill yo' cat.

Spider bring money,
Spider bring luck.
If yo' kill a spider,
All yo' life yo' will work.

Cry, cry baby,
Wallow, wallow dumpling,
Push yo' finger in yo' eye,
An' tell your mother it was I.

WE DON'T CARE!

Children, children,
 Yes, Mamma.

Where yo' been to?
 Gran Mamma.

What she give yo'?
 Two apples.

Where yo' put them?
 On the shelf.

Suppose they fall?
 We don't care.

I'll beat yo' tonight.
 We'll tell Pappa!

*As the children answer Mamma, they get nearer and
nearer until finally Mamma turns and chases them.*

BACK HOME

Johnny was a maker,
Live in Jamaica.
Had three daughters,
Name Jamaica.
Jump through the window,
Broke m' little finger.
Timba timba,
Inganglo.
Bend down low,
Inganglo.
Me Mamma broke m' toe,
Inganglo.
Fela, fela,
Inganglo.

TIME FOR BED

Baby mine, oh baby mine,
Now go to sleep;
Close your little sleepy eyes
And dream sweet dreams.

Dodo, petit po-po,
Mamma coming just now;
Dodo, petit po-po,
Mamma coming just now.

ENDINGS

Fall on de wire,
De wire bend;
And that's the way,
The story end.

Cric Crac,
Monkey break he back,
For a rotten pomerac.

A pomerac is a fruit.